Underneath the Lintel

Underneath the Lintel

An Impressive Presentation of Lovely Evidences

by Glen Berger

With an Afterword by the Playwright

Stage & Screen
New York

Acknowledgments

My thanks and gratitude extend to dozens of people who have been involved with the play during its incarnations, but there are several who are more or less responsible for keeping the play out of the birdcage, where, at times, it may have made a very nice floor covering.

Randy White not only directed the awfully gratifying New York production, he also made invaluable suggestions after the 1999 Yale Cabaret, and is the one who suggested that I *not* simply stick the thing in a desk drawer for the next twenty years as I was seriously considering. Brian T. Finney, T. Ryder Smith, and David Chandler have all delivered exquisite performances, enriching the final version of the text, and finding depths and nuances in the character I hardly knew existed. The producers of the Off-Broadway production—Dana Matthow, Tom Wirtshafter and Scott Morfee—committed themselves to the play in a way I had no right to expect, and my gratitude to them knows no bounds. Also many thanks to the Manhattan Theatre Club, who sponsored a reading of the play for their "Six at Six" series in 2000. Deep wells of gratitude to my agent Joyce Ketay and her assistant Kirsten Bowen, and also to Liz Duffy Adams. And of course and most of all, to my wife, Karin Almquist—muse, sounding board, and, most importantly, *editor*.

Notes on Setting and Character

Set

The Librarian has rented the space for the night, and from what we know of the Librarian, we can assume he didn't have much to spend for it. Perhaps the auditorium we're in has been dark for some time, or perhaps the theatre is "between shows." Props and other detritus from other shows can litter the back of the stage, or be seen in an exposed back room. An air of dilapidation wouldn't be a bad thing. I've always pictured the Librarian as delivering this lecture in a not-so-good part of town, on a rainy night, to perhaps only four or five down-and-outs more interested in getting dry from the rain than listening to a lecture by a Dutchman. Over the course of the evening, however, the "lecture" should imperceptibly turn into "theatre." The detritus, unnoticed and seemingly unimportant at first, can unexpectedly take on significance, alluding to scenes and history mentioned in the play. The lighting can become warmer, more "theatrical," etc., and what seemed like a random strewing of objects, or a random water stain on the wall, for instance, can turn out to be not so random after all.

Character

Why a Dutchman? The Dutch (to make an entirely unsupported generalization) have a wonderfully bureaucratic streak in them. They also tend to have a remarkable facility for other European languages. Most of all, I have known more than one person from the Netherlands whose English was remarkable, and whose accent was nearly imperceptible. (I also just have a soft spot for the Dutch.) My point is that the accent should be very light, and the actor should pay more attention to the "idiolect," meaning "an individual's unique way of speaking." (In fact, the tone and cadences of the Librarian were inspired less by any Dutch person, and more, if anywhere, from the patter of English music hall comedian Dan Leno, who performed at the turn of the century.) The Librarian is an utter novice to the stage, but perhaps a part of him is enjoying the privilege (and he paid for the privilege after all) of actually treading the boards.

Production History

Underneath the Lintel was first presented at the Yale Summer Cabaret, in New Haven, Connecticut, for three nights in August 1999, with the author playing The Librarian.

Underneath the Lintel was produced by The Actors' Gang in Los Angeles for a limited run in May 2001. It was directed and designed by Brent Hinkley; produced by Patti McGuire; stage-managed by Byrne Lethnik. The cast was as follows:

The Librarian Brian T. Finney

Underneath the Lintel premiered Off-Broadway at the Soho Playhouse, officially opening on October 23, 2001, and produced by Scott Morfee, Tom Wirtshafter, and Dana Matthow. It was directed by Randy White; set design was by Lauren Helpern; projection design consultant was Elaine McCarthy; lighting design was by Tyler Micoleau; sound design was by Paul Adams; costume was by Miranda Hoffman; the production stage manager was Richard Hodge; and the production coordinator was Cris Buchner. The cast was as follows:

The Librarian T. Ryder Smith

In January 2002, David Chandler took over the role of The Librarian.

Underneath the Lintel

Underneath The Lintel

(Stage contains a chair [which should never be used for sitting], a large chalkboard [to be used at director's discretion]. There is also a battered screen for showing slides, the slide projector to be operated by the actor. A Rather Old And Disheveled Man in decrepit suit shuffles onto the stage carrying a battered suitcase full of scraps. The suitcase, once open, may have various homemade contrivances to display the "evidences." [Perhaps he also keeps certain evidences in his pockets, with evidence tags dangling out.] He wears a date-stamper tied with string around his neck.)

LIBRARIAN

So. Right. We'll proceed. I have only one night for this . . . I'd like to have more, oh yes, but due to the extortionary rates demanded by the proprietors of this auditorium . . . I have only one night for this. Still. We'll proceed. *(he points significantly to suitcase he has set down)* Box of scraps. *Significant* scraps. Or rather . . . they're all I have . . . to *prove a life* . . . To prove one life . . . and justify another . . . and if you're thinking "that's a tall order for a box of scraps," well just you wait. *(with ominous significance)* They're not just scraps. *(announcing) An Impressive Presentation of Lovely Evidences.* Hold on to your hats, gentlemen. Bonnets, ladies. Hold on . . . *(scanning seats)* is this all there is? I don't know what more I can do! I put up signs, I did, on the poles, "Impressive Presentation!" but as soon as I turn my back, they're plastered over! With other signs! And mine were nicer. And important. And tomorrow, I'll be gone . . . *(pondering it on a more personal level—)* . . . in no time at all . . . I'll be gone *(but pulls himself out of it)* . . . Still. We'll proceed.

I am . . . a librarian. From Hoofddorp, that's Holland. Or rather, I was, before I was fired. Or rather, I retired. Against my will. Without my pension. Or rather, that's no concern of yours. Or rather, it will be, but not yet. My special duty for more than many years being to check in the books that came in overnight through the overnight slot. In the back of every book, you see, there's a little envelope, and in this little envelope, there's a little card, and on that little card . . . *the little date the book is due.*

(holds up stamper) This is my stamper. Oh yes, I wasn't letting them keep this. It's lovely—it contains every date there ever was. You don't believe me? *(closes eyes, fiddles with stamper dials)* "August 27, 1883," . . . there, that's the date Mount Perboewaten explodes in Krakatoa, 36,000 people perish under the ash. It's all in here! All the trials and joys of history. *(closes eyes,*

fiddles with dials) "January 25, 1971" . . . oh, January 25, 1971 . . . Helen . . . Shattock is walking her dog in Dayton when a frozen block of urine from the lavatory of a Pan Am jet falls, and hits her on the head, killing her instantly. Mind you *(fiddles with stamper)*, same date, "1836," Cetewayo, King of the Zulus is born! Oh yes, this stamper contains every birth in this room, not just Cetewayo's. And death. Yes, our deaths too . . . somewhere . . . My death is in here . . . somewhere . . . I just don't know . . . where . . . Still. Gives you a bit of respect for it, doesn't it. The stamper.

So. Yes. So, each and every day I woke up, took the bus, no, no wife, no children, I lived alone, got to the bibliotheque, put my labeled lunch in the employees icebox, gave a but-just-perceptible nod to Brody van Brummelen, works in reference fine fellow I'm sure except that I'm sure that he's not and always angling for the acquisitions position that by all rights is mine, that is, I'm next in line!, em, arrived at my desk, yes that's next, quieted the patrons with a well-timed "ssh" and advanced the date on my little stamper . . . one notch.

Now listen, the overnight slot is strictly for those books *not overdue*. But we checked anyway. That was my job. To check. Now and then you'd find a book a day or two overdue. Sometimes a week. Once, it is said, a book was returned, in the *slot* mind you, three months overdue—well we got over it, but we weren't amused. And neither was the violator when he saw the fine ho ho. Still. We'll proceed.

One morning *(he writes "1986" on the chalkboard)*, one fine and miserable and typical morning, nothing to give an inkling of what was to come—*(significantly)* I found this book in the pile. *(he takes out a battered book from the box with a tag attached to it labeled "Evidence #1")* We'll label it Eveydence #1. It is a Baedeker's travel guide, in deplorable condition. Well, I was just about to give the little card my stamp with the old stamper when my eyes suddenly sprang out of my head and rolled about on the floor and under the table. And why? Because I saw that this book was checked out in *1873* and no . . . no— never returned till it was returned. Do you understand? *(he writes "1873" on the chalkboard)* That's 113 years . . . overdue! Astounded out of my wits I was. It must have been his great-great grandson returning the book, a blot on the family only now being remedied. And in the overnight slot no less! Appalling. If you have a book 113 years overdue . . . you go to the counter, you admit your lapse, you pay the fine. Well, he wasn't getting away with it, not a chance, I checked the files—oh yes, we keep all the files, and I found the page and here it is. *(he takes out a page from a ledger labeled)* "Eveydence #2." *(reads)* "Baedeker's Travel Guide, checked out November 12th, 1873 by capital A . . . period." *(writes "A." on chalkboard)* That's his name. Capital A. Period. About as vague as they come, but never mind, what's his address, so I can send him the fine of his life. *(reads)* "Post Office Box 121, Dingtao."

Well Dingtao didn't ring any bells so I got out the old atlas. *(he procures an atlas and pages through it)* I've always liked atlases. They allow you to travel all over the world—*without the expense.* Yes it's true, I had never left Holland. I had rarely left Hoofddorp. I went to Gouda once to see how they made the cheese. But the tour wasn't given that day, they were closed, so never mind. Here it is, Dingtao, near Kaifeng. And no, it seems Kaifeng is not near Hoofddorp. No. Nor Rotterdam. No. It's China! Now how a Chinaman managed to check out a book from a Dutch library without a residence in the Netherlands, well—that would be the first of many puzzlers in this twisty mystery of a tale. And was he even a Chinaman? After all, the notes scrawled in the margins of the book were written in every language under the sun. Including Welsh. Well, it was none of my business. I filled out the standard form notifying our man of the pretty fine awaiting him, and bunged it off to China, and that was that.

But was that really that? No. That was not in any way . . . that. I couldn't get the miscreant out of my mind. I didn't reshelve the book, no, I thumbed through it. I took it home with me. I carried it about. And one day as I was flipping through it, I came upon this. *(pulls from book)*

Eveydence #3. Bookmark. But not just any book-mark. No. A bookmark *by proxy*. An unre-deemed claim ticket for one pair of trousers left in a Chinese laundering establishment. Oh, in China? No. In London. In *(writes on chalkboard) 1913*, seventy-three years previous.

Well. My life went on, the bus, the books, the "how are you today, Brody," and "no, I don't think my lunch is taking up too much room in the ice box, Brody, no, well, I'm sorry you feel that way," and the organizing of the cart and a "have a good night yourself" and then off with the lights and home again, but I'll say this . . . I got to thinking about those trousers. In fact, I couldn't *stop* thinking about those trousers. In fact I had more than one *dream* about those trousers, Trousers, Trousers, Trousers, Trousers until I couldn't take it anymore. Never claimed! Oh sure, the shop probably went defunct years ago, but perhaps . . . not! Anyway I was loath to fritter away my vacation days just to go to London for some nonexistent trousers . . . so I *applied* to travel to London on *library business—* to claim the trousers you see on behalf of the library to recoup some of the losses the library would no doubt accrue from the unpaid fine. It was the most daring gambit I had ever devised, but I felt I was on solid ground, and what do you know, the application was . . . rejected. Flat out. With a reprimand attached about "frivolous requests." Oh I was beside myself and I did a bit of inconspicuous sulking, and also some very discrete running up and down the stacks up and down in a frenzy . . . until I was calm again . . . But damn it to hell, I still couldn't get the pants out of my head, so I went to London all the same.

(we hear the 1930s tune "Life Begins at Oxford Circus" or similarly jaunty '30s-vintage tune from an English "sweet" band)

. . . expending . . . precious . . . vacation . . . time.

(and we see slides of London as—) London. Dear God the Chaos! The bustle! Oh this was a terrible mistake, why wasn't I home in Hoofddorp in front of the goggle box, cup of tea, nothing ever on but I didn't mind, tall red buses and sweet shops run by Pakistanis—and not very good sweets at that—and I watched the changing of the guard till I had to be changed myself, and the Bloody Tower and the Roman Wall and to think this all used to be swamps and mastodons. "What's this? Something for the French tourist—*Les Misérables*—that looks

interesting—"the miserable"—"It's all about me in London," I thought, and I had never seen a play before, so I paid, and it's true, after two hours, I was more *"misérables"* than I had ever been before. Still, we'll proceed.

To the Holloway Road and the Chinese laundry and . . . well what do you know, it was still there. The shop. So I strode in, waved around my claim ticket, and I came out with a pair of trousers. *(from the box he extrudes—)* Eveydence #4. Trousers. And never cleaned in all that time because they were in such a state of disrepair to begin with. A common laundry policy it seems, to protect the shop from accusations of negligence, I was the gladder for it, because it meant that any clues would be left *in situ* as they say.

And I was rewarded. I checked the pockets and I found . . . this. *(he extrudes from pocket with evidence tag attached—)* A used tram ticket.

Eveydence #5. From *1912*. A tram that ran in Bonn. Ger-ma-ny.

> *(and we hear the tune "Ungarwein" by von Geezy and his Orchestra [or similarly vaguely Germanic '30s-vintage upbeat and librarian-inspiring tune; a song by the Comedian Harmonists, e.g.] and see a slide of Bonn and the Municipal Transportation Headquarters)*

Well I don't know what got into me, feverish, I took a bus to Bonn, to the Municipal Transportation Headquarters to read up on incident reports for the month of March 1912. Oh yes, I was a regular detective now. It was a shot in the dark, I know, but I figured any scofflaw making loose with the library rules might have made some trouble on a tram in Bonn as well. Well you never know. And hey ho, look at what I found. *(he takes out from his box—)* A photeystat I'll label #6, and reads, in the German, as written by the tram conductor, as follows—

"*Ein Mann mit einem Bart und einem neu—*" *(stops short, to audience—)*

"*Sprechen sie*"—oh, no, yes of course . . . em, let's see . . . *(and he translates—)*

"A man with beard and curious hat and smelling truly foul, boarded the tram at Potsdamer Platz with a mangy dog. Although there were plenty of seats, he *refused to sit,* and instead paced up and down the aisle with his dog distracting the other passengers and myself. A dirty Jew, I threw him off at Wittlesbach."

Well, surely this wasn't the same man as the man who owned these trousers, but there was a chance, slim, and I was hooked. And I hated it! What was I doing in Bonn, sauerkraut gives me . . . *(he's said too much and now it's too late)* . . . well . . . flatus. Wind. Yes, it's a . . . problem . . . *(quickly turning to Baedeker's)* Bonn, devastated by the Normans, rebuilt, devastated by Frederick III, rebuilt, devastated yet again in World War II . . . rebuilt! In a chocolate shop I knocked over an enormous display of marzipan and by the end of the day, it was . . . rebuilt. Moved to tears by the humanity of it all. The persistence, the forbearance. Or I would have been, if "A Period" hadn't kept doing the backstroke across my brain, who is he! No no, I needed a distraction. Quick—I ducked into a playhouse, showing a play called *(perplexed and dismayed)* . . . *Les Misérables*. It was exactly the same. Only worse. And it was no distraction! The tram, the trousers, the travel guide, I had to find out more about this man! But how? A dead end it seemed. "Curious hat" "smelling foul" "threw him off at Wittlesbach" Hang on. What's that about a dog. *(draws a dog on the chalkboard)* He had a dog, it said, in Germany, in 1912. And he was in England in *1913* long enough to drop off his trousers. But! For the past one hundred years, there's been a law in England—all dogs from foreign countries must be put in quarantine *(draws prison cell around dog)* for six months on the grounds of Rabies Prevention, there being no rabies in England. Could it be then that our man was forced to leave his dog in English quarantine? Because, if so, there would be records! I called in to Hoofddorp extending my vacation, ignored the grumblings on the other end, worried a little about giving Brody the one-up but I'd attend to that, and like a shot, I was back on British soil, rifling through files for dogs deposited between March 1912 and November 1913, and here was something very curious— Only one dog, stay with me here, one dog alone, was put in quarantine during that period, who, after six months, was not reclaimed. That dog's name was . . . *(writes on chalkboard)* . . . Sabrina . . .

(we hear a scratchy recording of "It's a Long Way to Tipperary" [preferably by John McCormack] [or similar World War I-vintage war song] and see a slide of soldiers in trenches)

Sabrina. October 1914 and Sabrina still not claimed. World War I had started by then, ten million men would be slaughtered by the end, and the German dog, Sabrina, she too was put down, at last . . . Gassed . . . And as I stood there in that office, I began to wonder . . . *(looks about)* What was I doing here?! But! And yet! what was that dog doing here. And what was anybody doing in those trenches in 1914— *(to slide of soldier)* oh but you doughboys had a song for that, didn't you, how did it go—

(sings waveringly the old soldier song [to tune of "Auld Lang Syne"]—)

"We're here because we're here because we're here because we're here . . ." Yes, well enough of that.

The veterinarian's report on Sabrina is a tear-jerker and reads in part— *(reading scrap of paper with evidence label dangling on it)* "This dog was brought to us with its footpads torn to shreds. And yet, when we told the dog to sit, it whined and whimpered, and refused to sit, and cowered in terror, as if sitting would bring with it a terrible beating." Poor Sabrina! And remember now, our man in the tram was reported as pacing up and down, *refusing to sit.* Well. This was getting interesting. *(apologizing to audience)* Not riveting. But interesting. And nothing else of note except this, Except this!— *(reveals, attached to the report, with its own evidence tag)* a release statement, handwritten by our Mister Mystery, oh yes, matching to a tee all the loops of the ells and ees that we have here in the margins of the bloody Baedekers! And he signed it—*"A" period.* And he wrote, "I give full authorization to these fellows to keep for the proscribed allotment of time, my dog, *Zebrina.*" Not Sabrina. But "Ze." With a Z, E. Zebrina. Well. "What sort of a name is that?" I wondered. So I looked it up in the dictionary, and encyclopedia, and one of those "name-the-baby" books and do you know what I found? Nothing. Still. I tucked it away in the back of the thinking thing that I cleverly carry around with me, sometimes, and there was this too—our man was required on this form to leave the name and address of a man in the country who could vouch for him, and he wrote "The estate of the Lord of Derby, Attention: Thomas Wright."

And here's where things take a turn. And I'm talking about my stomach, for one. And here's why. I did a bit of research. Thomas Wright did live on the estate of the Lord of Derby, oh yes, but it was **almost two hundred years previous to the date of the Release Statement, Thomas Wright lived on the estate of the Lord of Derby from 1720 to 1754.** *1754.* Two hundred and thirty-two years before the Baedeker's book was returned. Well this didn't make any sense. I was a bit scared now . . . no one lives that long . . . surely . . . surely . . . he wrote down the first name that came to his head, having no one truly who could vouch for him in England. . . . Surely! but if you think I wasn't up in Derby the next day, to the archives now overseen by the National Trust, sifting through the account books of Thomas Wright, well, you'd be wrong. This was getting funny, and I didn't like it.

Eveydence #9. A page from Wright's Account Book. Whose now? Thomas Wright's. He kept the accounts of the estate of the Lord of Derby. How many chamber pots ordered and whatnot. And a diligent man was he. And good for us. And here's why. Year, 1748. Page 112, line 8— "Earthstopper—hired for week. Four pence." So what? So this—in the margins next to the line, and on the back of the page, Wright scribbled the following—

(and the Librarian acts out the following in
a clearly rehearsed, but rather stiltedly ren-

*dered, performance [though still managing
to impart an air of mystery to "the man in
the funnel-shaped hat"]—)*

"Whilst riding in coach, early evening, encountered a most curious man wearing faded yellow funnel-shaped hat roaming grounds of estate. 'Sir,' I said, 'You are trespassing on private ground belonging to the Lord of Derby, you don't belong here.'

"'I *don't* belong here, I don't belong anywhere at all, but I'm everywhere nonetheless and you can thank your Lord for that.'

"'Do you have a grievance with my Lord?'

"'You don't know the half of it,' he replied, in an accent impossible to place, but if I had to venture, I would say half-French, half . . . monkey.

"'May I ask how my Lord has grieved you, sir?'

"'You may ask, but I mayn't answer—I'm not allowed to tell you how he has wronged me.'

"'Then how do you expect my Lord of Derby to make amends,' I said, rather exasperated. And here, the curious man doubled over, and said that was the funniest joke he had ever heard. He said evidently we have been talking about two different Lords. Well, obviously an escapee from Bedlam, but suddenly remembering that I was in desperate need of an earthstopper for tomorrow's hunt, I took the liberty of asking this crooked man if he would like a night's employment. At the word 'earthstopper,' his eyes lit up."

Hold on. Stop the narrative. What's earthstopping. Well, let's look it up. *(we see a slide of Joseph Wright's nineteenth-century painting "The Earthstopper")* Oh yes, here's a picture of it and a faded miserable picture it is. Apparently it's a little tactic developed by the foxhunting gentry.

Foxes, apparently, live in dens, snug little places . . . At night, the foxes leave their dens, and skulk about, looking for supper. Otherwise, it's the dens for them. Well, if you live on a big estate, and you're throwing a foxhunting party in the morning, you don't want all the foxes in their dens, no. Your guests will say, one and all, "well that was a lousy party." So what do you do. You employ an *earthstopper*, who goes out with his lantern and spade the night before, and while the fox is out, he stops up his den right up to the top with earth. When the fox returns, he can't find his home. "What miserable earthstopper's done this," says the fox, "burying my wife and all my lovelies, and now I must roam the hills till morn and find a fix to this conundrum." And, of course, in the morn—while the fox is aroaming—the dogs, the horns, the horses, the slaughter. Lovely. Now back to the narrative.

"...At the word 'earthstopper,' his eyes lit up. 'Oh, are you one who appreciates a good hunt?'

"'Well no, I like the idea of the little fox roaming about with no place to return to—it's ... funny.'

"As he appeared exhausted I bade him ride in the coach, which he did, but he would not sit. When I insisted he sit, he insisted with equal force he would not. Unable to abide by a man who insists on standing stooped in front of me in a coach, I bade him walk on behind until ..."

And here the little anecdote suddenly and forever stops, the next page missing, you see ... Thomas Wright, you see, grew liquidy in the mind, over time, and the little children would steal in, and steal his official papers to use for kites, and the life of Wright got snagged in trees and down drainpipes. *(with unexpected bitterness)* And whose doesn't.

But! We have this. A man who wouldn't sit on a coach, a man who wouldn't sit on a tram, a man's dog who wouldn't sit in a kennel, a man with a grievance against some lord, and a man with a funny hat. Well. I'm no mathematician, but even I could see that it was beginning to add up. *(beat)* Not that I was bad in mathematics, mind you. Next to Rosa van der Werff, I was top in my class, for a year. And that's where I met her actually. Rosa. In math. Oh she had a wonderful brain for . . . what are those things . . . variables. We'd do our homework after school, that's how it started. Fine old time though—giggling, of all things . . . I wasn't even supposed to be in her class but I was transferred over, heaven knows why . . . *(now intensely introspective)* . . . there's a thought for you . . . *(and comes out of it when he notices the audience)* Oh, yes, well enough of that, em, look at this.

(We see a slide projected—) This is a page from a fourteenth-century German manuscript, depicting a man with a yellow funnel-shaped hat. He's of the Hebraic faith. How do I know? Because all men of the Hebraic faith had to wear a funny hat just like this one. *In the fourteenth century*, that is. All of this weighed heavily on the mind as I returned to the day–to–day in Hoofddorp. I stamped, oh yes, I filed, I fined, but *inside* the brains were churning like the machinery in a cheese factory. When it *isn't* closed. I had clues, eveydence, but what did it mean? The patrons were noisy, I didn't care, overdue books came in, I didn't care, someone stole my lunch from the icebox, I . . . cared, but not as much as I would have.

And then, one day, *it happened.* I was manning the information desk, when I received an urgent call, ring ring, from a patron inquiring about the amount of direct sunlight one should allow a Zebra Plant. Well I got out the handy reference guide to houseplants, turned to the index, looked up Zebra Plant, and what do you think I saw right below it? "Zebrina!" With a Z, E. As in the dog! "Zebrina Pendula. Page 130." Surely it meant absolutely nothing, but I flipped violently to the page all the same and there at the top *(and he reads in his houseplant book—),* "Zebrina Pendula, Latin for the common houseplant Tradescantia" . . . and then . . . a shiver . . . for in parentheses . . . "also known as . . . the Wandering Jew . . ."

I swallowed hard. For in a little-used musty little corner of my head, I remembered hearing something once about a myth of a Wandering Jew. Oh Great Guns! In a flash I dashed to the card catalog, and "move out of my way, Brody," and "damn it, Brody, this is *more* important," and "oh wouldn't *you* like to know," and "scramoosh, scramoosh, goodbye, scramoosh" . . . made sure the coast was clear . . . looked up "W" for "Wandering" *(taps head)* . . . and found it! *(and he demonstrates a tattered library catalog card)* "Tales of the Wandering Jew."

As the story goes, and it's been going for centuries, there once was a cobbler, a Jew, kept to himself, never married, stayed out of trouble, living in Judea, around 36 anno domini, although no one in the world knew it was 36 anno domini . . . not knowing there was a *dominus* in their midst to make it anno domini. And can you blame them. Would *you* recognize a miracle if you saw one? What if you think, "Oh, I'll never see a miracle." Or what if you think, "Well at least I'm sure I haven't seen one yet." What if . . . you're wrong?

It was April, hot day it was in Judea, the

smells of the Pesach meal the night before still lingering, and he, our Jewish cobbler, at work with awl and lace, in his little shop, on a shoe—when there was a terrific shouting and haroo outside his window. He went out on his front step and there on the street, a procession of soldiers and convicted men toting their crosses, no doubt to Golgotha. The cobbler had seen it all before, and had little to say about it—like I said, he minded his own affairs. When suddenly, one of the frailest and sorriest of the convicted lot collapsed, right there, right on the steps, right by the door of our cobbler. The name of the collapsed man was Yeshua, and he was a mess. "Well. What do I do," thought the cobbler. Underneath the lintel he stood. The lintel. The top of the doorframe. He stood under it. Yes? Good. Underneath the lintel he stood. Not lentil . . . *lintel.* You have to understand this or all is lost. Underneath the lintel he stood, and tussled with his quaking brain. "Let him lie on your step a minute, let him catch his breath, it can do no harm." But already the Roman soldiers were pressing this Yeshua to get up, and telling the cobbler to cease in this aiding and abetting or he'd have to answer for it himself *with a cross of his own!,* and the cobbler was shot through and through with fear, he had a great fear of the law, you see, and a greater fear of death, and his hands were forced besides, and he thought, "I don't know this Yeshua, he's probably a thief, a murderer even, although he doesn't look like a murderer, but a troublemaker no doubt," and this was trouble the cobbler could do without, so he says to this Yeshua, he says to this man with the cross . . . "get off my step . . . go on . . . move on . . . enough tarrying . . . do your resting some-where else!" . . . And this Yeshua did get up, calm-

ly, and turned to the cobbler and said—"I will go
. . . but you, you will tarry till I come again."

And off he went, and there we go, and the
cobbler didn't think twice about that little
episode, and he lived to be an old man and knew
his end was near, which was fine by him, by now
he was sick of living. He got ill . . . wrote out his
will . . . and then . . . he got well. Lived a few more
years, got sick again, called everyone to his bed-
side . . . and then . . . fie upon it, he got well again.
And then he began to notice an even curiouser
phenomenon. He noticed, upon reaching the age
of eighty, that instead of appearing older, he was
looking, well, younger. And he suddenly got the
urge to go for a walk, and he left his house and
was never seen by his family again.

For fifty years he lived in this vagabond state,
incognito, getting younger all the while, and
then, he started to get older again, which went

on for fifty years, and then, younger again, and
fifty years of that, and on and on, older, younger,
older, younger. And by this time there was more
than a little groundswell claiming that this man
Yeshua with the cross was more than he seemed
to be, indeed . . . indeed, that he was the son of
God . . . of all things . . . and that He would come
again at the end of days as the long-awaited
meshiach, and the cobbler hearing these
rumours began to put two and two together,
what was it that that Yeshua said? "I will go, but
you, you will tarry till I come again," Holy
Scamander, it all made sense to him now. He was
going to be stuck on this lousy old earth until the
Second Coming. "So there was a God after all,"
he thought. Well that's Good. And God had it in
for him specifically. Not good. Bad. Really awful.
For over time, this Jew discovered two stipula-
tions of this unique curse which made the thing

more than unbearable. One—that he may never rest. Physically impossible for him. That means never sleep. Never lie down. Never sit down. Never kneel. Could he lean? A little. But just a little. So that's one stipulation, and not very nice— I mean . . . sitting down . . . it's a wonderful thing, a little rest, when you're exhausted, it isn't asking much, and if you're not allowed to sit, you become *beyond* exhausted, you just want to stop, for a moment, and if you can't stop, then at least crawl, on your knees, but if you're not allowed to crawl, then you just want to die, and if you're not allowed to die . . . It's grisly. But Number Two Stipulation is just as worse, in a way, and it's this—the Jew *can never identify himself.* He is never allowed to confirm his own existence to his fellow man. He can be nothing more than a myth, whether he's a myth or not.

Now then. Let's get one thing absolutely

clear. The Wandering Jew *is* a myth. Not the houseplant, mind you. No— *(we see a slide of houseplant)* This is a picture of the houseplant, and as you can see, the tendrils are, shall we say, wandering, from the pot, yes, and so it became known as the Wandering Jew. And this is a picture of it. And it's mine. A documented photeygraph of the Wandering Jew zebrina pendula houseplant. I do not have a documented photeygraph of the Wandering Jew *Jew*. Everyone knows after all that it's just a myth. A myth. As in God is a myth. As in that old myth that life has any meaning or significance. A myth. But more and more I was becoming convinced that although the Wandering Jew was just a myth, I was in possession . . . of that myth's . . . *pants.*

The woman on hold . . . waiting to hear about her Zebra Plant . . . was, regrettably, forgotten, completely. That is, until the next day

when she sent a letter of complaint to my superiors—I, who had never received a complaint in
my life! Oh it made dear Brody's month, I don't
know how he found out about it. He even gave
me a chocolate for consolation. *(steeped in bitterness)* I didn't need his chocolate. *(clarifying)* I
ate it, but I didn't need it. So yes . . . yes . . . it was
becoming clear that this overdue book was
beginning to interfere . . . with my work . . . And
yet I couldn't stop thinking about it!

Because . . . what if he did exist. . . . I mean, a
man *(perhaps draws a man on the chalkboard)*
living immortally, incognito, somewhere on this
earth, well that's odd enough, but if he existed, it
meant something even odder existed too . . . God
. . . *God* . . . And all the irate Zebra Plant owners
and reference department rivals in the world
suddenly seemed . . . a little less important than
they did before . . . I used to lose sleep over them

. . . Now I lost sleep over something else . . . Mr. A period. Oh yes, I forgot to mention another confounding coincidence—that in more than one source, the name of the Wandering Jew is *Ahasuerus,* do you see? Ahasuerus. As in "please initial the rental contract here, here and here Mr. Ahasuerus." "Righteeo—A period, A period . . . A Period!"

Well. I got to thinking. If I were in such a predicament, in which a superior had foisted an unreasonable condition upon me, well there's two ways you can go, either (a) accept your new condition grovelingly, or (b) find a way around it. I've always been more of the option (a) sort of man. If you can call that a man. But what if you've been practicing option (a) for over a thousand years, and now you're getting a little weary of it? A superior makes an unreasonable demand—in this case—your life, your history,

your trials and suffering, can never be authenti-
cated, or even communicated, no, no, after a
thousand years, "option (b)" begins to look better and better—find a way around it. Trousers,
claim tickets, incident reports—what if these
things weren't as incidental, as accidental, or
casual and trivial as they *seemed*. Just hypothe-
tically speaking, you're the hypothetical
Wandering Jew. Well wouldn't *you* drop little
clues, from time to time, nothing overt mind
you, nothing to catch His notice, but just little
things . . . like . . . oh, I don't know . . . conve-
niently leaving your *pants*, for instance. . . . Or
taking out a discrete post office box in China.
(*slaps hand to forehead*) China! Of course! The
man has a post office box in China! If I really
wanted to settle this once and for all, be done
with this nonsense, all I had to do was go to
China. But! I mean . . . China . . . that seemed just

a little bit further away than, say . . . Neptune. *(drawing a brain on the chalkboard)* I put my brain under some good hard scrutiny—it had been playing fast and loose for too long and it needed an audit. *(speaks to drawing—)*

"Brain! What in heaven's name are you doing to me? Do you truly believe that this mysterious man is—"

"No!" says the brain, "certainly not . . . or . . . oh . . . I don't know anymore . . ."

. . . thus spoke the brain . . . thus began the beginning of the end . . . because I felt myself more and more believing . . . I who had never believed anything in my life! *Accepted,* oh yes, I accepted plenty. But the act of *accepting* and the act of *believing* are two very different things. What was happening to me now, was a very different thing indeed. . . . A book drops into my lap one morning. Was it just an overdue book . . . or a *challenge* . . . Would *I* recognize a miracle if I saw one. . . ?

And yet No, this was mad mad mad mad mad. Back to my desk, stamp stamp away, turn the notch one each day and forget about it. What was I going to do, spend all my money to go to China! I, who had Hunan Chicken, once, Once! . . . and got the runs for a week! . . . And there was this too . . . my superiors wouldn't look kindly at any more gallivanting any time soon. The overnight slot was still clogged with piled up books, and even though I had plenty of vacation time left, I was forced to sit if I had any desire to keep my job . . . And so . . . I got ill. Oh yes, a cough, a sneeze, a swoon, and I was sent home. But . . . *(confiding)* it was all a ruse! I wasn't sick at all, no!, but I had a week of sick leave to show for it! Oh clever librarian—had anybody ever thought of that before—*pretend* you're sick to get out of work—no, I don't think so, that's a new one in the books I bet . . . Well I took the plunge . . . *(now realizing the weight of what he's done)* . . . now take the leap . . . absurd, but no choice, it was off with you . . . to the land of rice, the Great Wall, and . . . rice.

(we hear some chinoiserie number of a 1920s/'30s vintage, e.g., "Limehouse Blues" [preferably by Ambrose and his Orchestra], and see a slide of an overcrowded Chinese city)

China! A billion people. In Beijing less than a day and I believed it. At least a billion. And yet, it's funny, I think the death of even a cricket is noticed because as far as I could tell, they keep them all in cages for pets. Back in Hoofddorp, a million insects are getting caught in a million balls of lint behind a million couches every day and dying and nobody knows. Mind you *(fiddles with dials of stamper)*, in 1887 in Honan, China, a flood—like that!—drownded three million people, three million! and no one in Hoofddorp batted an eye at that either, so the insects behind the couches shouldn't take it personally, that's just the way it is. It may have been three million and one people who drownded, by the way, but what's that one to anyone but that one. If it isn't someone you know, then it's all just . . . behind the couch. Which begs the question, if I snuffed it tomorrow, would anyone notice? Oh yes, plenty. Or rather, a few. Or rather, Brody. But in two hundred years, five hundred, ten thousand, will anyone care that *he* perished? No. Or any of us here? . . . No. Lord Harry, we're all behind the couch, mutely struggling with our lint . . . not a cheery thought. Standing in Jaiseng Road in

Beijing surrounded by a billion other souls can
do that to your thoughts, a diversion was needed, I tried to get tickets for a show in town called
... *Les Misérables*—yes, I like it, I admit it—but
I was mistakenly given tickets to the Peking
Opera instead, and I went, and ... I liked that too
... I didn't know what was happening to me ...
I had heard that travel broadened the mind but
at this rate I would need a sombrero soon. But
on to Dingtao, where I greased a palm, a very
easy thing to do in Dingtao, as if our man had
foreseen it all, and I obtained access to the Post
Office Box of Mister A period.

Inside ... was one letter ... *(he takes letter
from box with great anticipation, then opens it, to
great disappointment)* ... from me, informing
him of his pretty fine. *(then spots another letter)*
And one letter, and one letter! dated January 6th,
1906, and here it is, Eveydence #11, written to

our man by one Esther Gelfer. In Yiddish. And of all things . . . a love letter. An excerpt of which reads as follows—

"If you must know . . . I am in love with you. Hopelessly. You probably don't remember me, but I remember you. In our town of misery, you suddenly appeared, and whistling that *funny little song.*" Make a note of that. *(draws a musical note on the blackboard)* . . . "I had never seen you in Zabludow before that day two years ago, the day the man with the phoneygraph came to get our voices on that machine, but I was smitten— you were shy, and knew every language under the sun, and I invited you back to my embarrassing little room. I was young, I was confused and you gallantly refused to lie with me. You refused to even sit down, in fact, and you left in a hurry, in a sweat, nervously, endearingly, and left your jacket behind. At any rate, I know you are well-traveled, and I have emigrated to Amerikay and this is my address and if ever you wish to reclaim your jacket, it is here . . . and I am here . . . both of us . . . waiting . . ." lovely . . . *(strangely affected by the letter)* . . . lovely . . .

(he snaps out of it, and we see a slide with map of Zabludow and a slide of Polish protesters)

She must have left Zabludow after the Revolution of 1905, Radical Jews in Russia and Congress Poland joining anti-czarists demanding democratic elections, and czarist authorities instigating pogroms to divert the masses . . . heads chopped off to divert the masses . . . from their heads, I suppose. . . . Well I couldn't stop now. No time for fried rice, it was a slow boat to Amerikay for me, to seek Esther Gelfer . . . out!

*(and we hear "Yiddisher Charleston" by
the old Gilt-Edged Four, or an appropriate
klezmer tune of 1920s/'30s vintage)*

Well I got to New York. A slog and a half, but
I did it, I did it. Heart pounding, I looked up
addresses, made call after call, and at last do you
know what I found? That after being in New
York for a year and a month, Esther Gelfer
moved. To Australia. Shoot me through the eyes.

Well, feeling down, I thought about seeing a
play that night to cheer me up, a certain French
play, but I took in a concert instead, outside, it
was free and what the heck, and then I went
swing dancing, of all things—there's a revival
apparently— *(we hear romantic swing music, and
he gradually, haltingly, rediscovers his feet)* —and
I hadn't danced like that since . . . well since . . .

Rosa van der Werff was in my arms in Hoofddorp too many years ago . . . oh I was high as a kite that New York night, and I bored a Japanese couple senseless explaining the Dewey Decimal System while we shared a horse and buggy through Central Park at midnight, oh it was capital T Wonderful. I mean Thrilling. Both. And. In the morning I jamfled over to the YIVO Institute for Jewish Research and its Archives of Sound Recordings and Photo Archives, oh yes, we librarians know just where to go for the references, and I unearthed this little item. *(we see a slide of a shtetl in 1904 with ethnographic surveyor with recording equipment)* Eveydence #13A—an ethnographic surveyor with recording equipment in *Zabludow* in April 1904. And do you know who that is, that gentleman to the left with his head just out of view? *(significantly)* Neither do I.

But! Eveydence #13B happens to be this—

(holds up a battered tape recorder [preferably quite out of date]) —a recording from an Edison cylinder *(also holds up an Edison cylinder),* one of the very ones made on that Zabludow day. Now listen.

(he plays tape, and we hear scratchy recording of person speaking Yiddish, with whistling very faintly in background)

That's Yiddish you're hearing, but listen harder. Do you hear that? In the background? That . . . whistling? What is that? Do you recognize it? It isn't a Polish folk song, no, nor a Jewish one neither, no. No, it's a little number entitled "When It's Nighttime in Italy"—*(sings)* "When it's Nighttime in Italy, It's Wednesday over here, When it's Fish Day in Germany, You can't get shaved in Massachusetts" etcetera. First recorded and released by Billy Jones and his Orchestra, in

New York in *April 1904! (significantly)* And now here it is, being whistled— *(perhaps circling drawing of man and the musical note)* —by some unidentified personage, in a tiny remote shtetl in Poland *the very same month!?* Well wouldn't it be just like our well-traveled man, as Esther writes, and I quote—to "whistle that funny little song" in the background thus ensuring that he would be recorded—incognito, but *in perpetuity*—that he would *leave his mark!*

Well it was on to Australia!, find Gelfer, I *had* to. And it was on the way, and only then, that I remembered something . . . I only had a week of sick leave . . . and I had been gone . . . *(figures in head)* a month and a half . . . I . . . was screwed. *(disturbed)* Still. We'll . . . proceed. We'll . . . proceed.

(we see a slide of Australia)

Australia, and what did I find. Dear Esther Gelfer. Dead. For thirty-five years. And what did I expect? A 121-year-old woman to answer all my questions? Yes. I did find a chest of Esther's effects *(indicating suitcase of scraps)*, there in the attic of her niece, now living outside Brisbane. Dear ... dead ... Esther Gelfer, there I stood ... amongst the ephemera of your life. *(more introspective)* There's a word. Ephemera. From "ephemeral"—short-lived—like those insects, the ephemerids *(draws a mayfly on the chalkboard)*, mayflies living a day and all to find their perfect mate, and then ... die ... *(he erases the mayfly)* ... Esther Gelfer ... never-married ... Did you live with regrets? "Settle down," you said to him. "Settle down" you said to a man who might have been the *Wandering Jew*, oh poor Esther ... Cupid *is* cruel ... or just blind and ignorant. If we're all cruel, it's just out of blind ignorance. Underneath the lintel . . . a cobbler told a man with a cross to shove on . . . and that made all the difference. *(suddenly, the Librarian seems overcome, voice cracking)* . . . Underneath the lintel . . . underneath the lintel . . . it's supposed to be an innocent place . . . where boys kiss their sweethearts good night . . . in the first bloom of love . . . Rosa van der Werff . . . wearing those eyes of hers . . . *(weeps)* she *did* love me . . . she said so . . . and what did I do? . . . and what did I do? . . . I must have been standing in an ice bucket—blazing heart . . . cold feet . . . *(pause)* and she married another . . . *(pause)* well you can't live with regrets . . . how was I to know she was the one . . . and only . . . *(fighting tears and losing)* no, move on . . . move on. . . . A . . . a . . . magician tells you to choose any card in the deck *(increasingly bitter)*, and so with free will you do choose ... but you don't realize the magician has subtly forced you to pick the exact card he wanted you to pick all along. Magicians call that a "Hobson's Choice." And in life we think we make choices ... but they're Hobson's Choices. So who is this Hobson? Who is this magician gulling us? That's the question. Simply something named Chance? Or Fate? *(looking up)* Or Something Else ...

(still fragile from breakdown) There in Esther's hope chest— *(pulls from box)* —a raggedy old jacket, and on the jacket, a faded yellow star, yes, like the type Jews were forced to wear in Augsburg *in the fifteenth century*, yes, and in the jacket—a coin. An old coin. A roman coin, from the time of Tiberius. Issued? 37 A.D. Eveydence? #16, underlined, circled, with exclamation points and arrows pointing to it!

(emotionally) That night, outside Brisbane, I

T. Ryder Smith in the Soho Playhouse production
Photo credit: Gilles Decamps

David Chandler in the Soho Playhouse production
Photo credit: Gilles Decamps

Brian T. Finney in the Actors' Gang production

Photo credit: Patti McGuire

". . . but look at the wings—there's words on them, a ghostly vestage" (*page 56*)

Photo credit: Reprint permission Glen Berger Collection

stared up at the stars until the old orbs watered— "how very . . . high they are . . ." Unreachable, that's the word . . . and a line from Job out of the blue blazed across the brain like a comet—"Hitherto shalt thou come . . . but no further . . ." But no, I'd have none of that talk. I was in for it now, Hobson knows I hadn't a choice, it was a world tour to track down this rapscallion, with the Baedeker's as my guide and clue-filled companion, for curse it all, if it's really him, then he lives, he lives!

(we hear the jaunty "Freilach Yidelach" by Dave Tarras [or a similarly spirited klezmer tune of '20s/'30s vintage by Tarras or Naftule Brandwein] as—)

(paging through Baedeker's, looking at margins)

Let's see, he knows German, and Italian . . . So I went to Germany, then Italy, then all over the world, where I found graffiti written in every language, including Welsh, and saying only this— *(writes on board or wall)* "I Was Here."

(we see slides of Acropolis and bathroom stall) To Greece, then France, and I found the words on the side of the Acropolis, and in a bathroom stall in the Paris Metro, "I was here," "I was here"— *(We see slides of Norwegian coast, totem pole, Mayan temple, etc.)* —on a rock in Norway, on a totem pole near Juneau, on the thirty-first step of a Mayan temple in Uxmal . . . on a park bench in Stamford, Connecticut, on a statue on Easter Island . . . "I was here," "I was here," "I was here" *(perhaps writes on wall)*, "I was here . . ."!

(Music out. Pause. And calmly—)

But you might say . . . "Yes, but look here . . .

those words could have been written by anyone. Perhaps you're not looking for the Wandering Jew at all, but Kilroy." And I would say to that . . . *(searches for answer, and finally flipping the bird with both hands at the audience, in exasperation)* . . . Fuck you! *(then sincerely shocked at his behavior—)* And then I would apologize *profusely*, and dig about in my box of scraps for some more tangible proof . . . *(thinks, eyes light up, and pulls from box, now a little uncomfortably frantic)* . . . Ah! Oh hoh! Look at this! Now look at this, look at this . . . Ripped from the Baedeker's . . . I took it from the Baedeker's . . . *(he holds up scrap with label dangling from it)* an illustration of the ruins in Rome. But by now I was learning to shift my focus, follow the blur in the periphery, look in the margins, the fringes, for that's where our man and The Truth have set up shop. So I peered very closely at the illustration of the ruins, and there in the corner, very small, a drawing of moths, for flavour . . . *(we see series of slides of the illustration, zooming in until we see the moths, with words on the wing—backwards—as if an impression from the page opposite)* . . . but look at the wings—there's words on them, a ghostly vestige—they must have come from the page opposite, from years of the two pages being pressed together—you see? yes? yes? yes?—but no!, the words don't correspond, so we can only assume that at one point a piece of paper had been inserted *between* the pages, and there was!, and I tracked it down!, and it's this!—a theatrical programme!, Eveydence #77, from the year 1777!, in *Holland*, for a performance entitled "The Wandering . . . *(reads surprised and profoundly deflated)* . . . Minstrel"? *(beat)* "Minstrel?" No. This said "Jew." This said "Jew." *(stares at paper in disbelief)* I swear to you, it was Jew. It said

Wandering Jew, I *saw* it . . . *(the Librarian, now
quite lost on the stage, reads, softly to self, working
hard to help himself make sense of this setback)*
"Wandering Minstrel" . . . *(Then—)* . . . Mind
you . . . there's a smoked herring . . . called a red
herring . . . that was used at one time to lay trails
to train hunting dogs, so the dogs could learn to
track the *aforementioned earthstopped fox.* Well.
For *advanced* training, the red herring was used
to *divert* the dog from the trail. All very confus-
ing for the dog but there's solace in this— A herring may have been a false herring, but every
false herring still *had its purpose. (perhaps looking at scrap then heavenward) There's never an
accidental herring,* oh no, every red herring,
every digression, is a step, perhaps a step sideways or backwards, but it keeps you moving
nonetheless . . . *(softly, perhaps realizing for first
time)* . . . and there's joy . . . too . . . in that . . .

Yes . . . yes, I was back in *Holland* to dig this one up. Strode into the Hoofddorp library, as if I hadn't been gone a day, Brody was head of acquisitions now, I almost felt sorry for him, chained to a desk all the day as he was. And after a few gawping stares from the library patrons, and some rather unkind remarks about the hum wafting off my unwashed self, I was called into the offices of my superiors and told . . . to shove on. *(humbled)* It was quite a blow. ". . . oh . . . well . . . oh . . . all right then . . . but what about my pension," I said. "Nothing doing," they said. "But . . . but then how will I manage? How will I enjoy a well-earned rest in my waning days?" "You won't. We're striking your name from the files, it will be as if . . . you were never here at all . . ." And I was shown out. And there on the steps, eating my chocolate from Brody, I stared in a daze from the other side of the door. At my old haunt, my second home. Underneath the lintel I stood, grappling with a thought. Yes? Should I? No? . . . Yes! And I marched back in, strode straight to my desk, stole my stamper, got out the sharpest letter opener I could find, and carved deep and irrevocably into my former desk so no one could ever be mistaken, "I WAS HERE . . . I WAS HERE." And then, oh boy did I run away, but fast.

Fine *(significance of losing job sinking in a bit)* . . . fine, I lost my job . . . *(now more desperate)* I lost my job . . . *(and full enormity hitting him)* I lost my job . . . *(clutches stamper, spluttering)* but I had the history of man in my hand, and, and, *(desperately)* I have this . . .

(and pulls from box an old horse brush [or some other antique worthless object]) This . . . is . . . a brush. *(stares at thing with ever-growing incomprehension)* Still. We'll Proceed.

(More desperately, he pulls from box, an item

in small pouch with label attached—) Ah! Look at this . . . look at this . . . this . . . now look at this . . . this this may *look* small and insignificant, but it is actually . . . the fossilized excrement of an ancient turtle. Oh yes. And you may ask, "what does this have to do . . . with the Wandering . . . Jew . . ." *(Long pause, as he stares at fossilized excrement. Looks all about the stage as if quite lost. All confidence in his scraps has now left him, and he says, softly.)* I don't know . . . I don't know . . . I don't know . . . gone . . . gone, the turtle goes . . . but leaves a testament more enduring than any of us can hope for . . . *(to excrement/audience)* . . . Do you know how Aeschylus died, that towering playwright of ancient Greece? It has to do with turtles. Apparently eagles pick up turtles and carry them aloft until they find a suitable rock to drop them on, to crack them open. One day, an eagle thought Aeschylus' bald head . . .

was a rock. Exit Aeschylus. And if you think "oh dear that's an awfully trivial death for such a grand person," not to worry—fourteen people in America die every year by vending machines falling on top of them. Vending machines—after shaking them for the fifty cents they just devoured . . . Life . . . fifty cents . . . *(bitterly despairing)* And it's not just the trivial deaths, no—all death has a way of making one's life, no matter how grand, seem silly and small—it's as if, as if Life were Beethoven's Ninth, but instead of culminating with a choir, a hundred-strong, it culminates with . . . the squeak of a dog toy. *(becoming increasingly agitated, bewildered, intensely bitter and tearful)* No, no Ode to Joy, nothing exalting, nothing exulting, just sense-lessness, senselessness, nothing miraculous, just a nuisance—Life, Love, Your One Love . . . your *one love . . . (pause) . . .* send her away . . . a mis-

take ... too late ... carry on as if it didn't matter
... It Did ... It *did* ... but now it doesn't
... for who can hear you, in no time at all you're
shunted off yourself and there you go—all's for-
given, if only because ... all's *forgotten* ... I used
to be a librarian ... what have I done ... I don't
know ... "To prove one life, and justify another
..." with scraps ... I'm sorry ... I'm sorry ... I'm
sorry ... *(he begins putting scraps back in the box,
and packing up, when suddenly he sees the World's
Fair recording in the box [either a shellac disc or a
cassette purporting to be a recording from the
record], picks it up, perplexed)* ... and yet ... to
say ... or yell out ... or carve in a wall, if but
once ... "*I was here* ..." well, there's this—last
scrap, I promise. ...

> *(and we see a slide of the World's Fair, and
> of the time capsule exhibit)*

At the 1939 World's Fair, in Queens, a time capsule was lowered, preserving all sorts of artifacts in a shell of titanium, to be unearthed a thousand years hence, a declamation of our little existence in the twentieth century. . . . Was our man there, being attracted to such a notion? *(pointing to photograph)* Is he somewhere in this crowd? Hard to say. But. There was a little booth at the Fair where you could make a record of yourself . . . for fifty cents. A few were left unclaimed. This *(holding up tape)* is a recording of one of them.

(and we hear on the tape a scratchy, and eerie, recording of an old man, perhaps slightly reminiscent of Librarian [with the Librarian echoing in a whisper "and yet . . ."])

"I am here . . . I am here . . . at the World's Fair . . . Is it? . . . Is the world fair? . . . Hardly . . . And yet . . . I'll say this . . . to any who can hear . . . I am here. . . . I am here. . . . I am here. . . . I am here. . . . I am here. . . ."

(and as the recording continues with numerous "I am here's," the Librarian, overlapping, sings slowly and softly, his eyes lighting up as a much-desired realization sinks in—)

"We're here because we're here because we're here because we're . . . here . . ."

(The recording fades out, and with a sort of beatific confidence—)

You don't have to believe me . . . Say I made

it all up . . . "He made it all up," I don't care anymore . . . I'm tired . . . Yes, I'm tired . . . but **I'm
not stopping my pursuit neither** . . . no . . . And
Why? Because I don't think Mr. A Period has
stopped, no, not given in, No, and never will.
And if one day He Above tells our man, at last,
that he may lie down . . . he'll sit. "Sit then," he'll
stand. "Stand then," he'll *walk. (God increasingly
angry/exasperated)* "Walk then," *he'll dance.* On
principle. No, no repentance, no—for in the
greatest act of defiance known to humankind,
our man *will* find a way, this I know, mark my
words, to behold this hash of a creation, to take
this muck and holy mess of a life, and winnow
out and revel in every bit of beauty and worth
that's in it so long as he's in it, so there. And so.
We Shall Proceed. Although . . . the trail trails off.
The last promising sighting of him was over fifty
years ago—testimony of a fellow doing a sort of

buck dance outside the fences at Buchenwald . . .
"The doomed souls within were probably deliri-
ous," you'll say . . . and what did they see after all
but a ragged Jew on the other side of the camp
fence . . . *But, you see, our man lives incognito* . . .
He could be there everywhere you look, but you
won't see him . . . If in Mexico, in a sombrero he'll
be. A kimono in Kyoto, a thong in New Guinea,
wooden clogs in Zander aan Zee . . . And I'll be
right there behind him . . . and after all these
years, both of us . . . beginning to learn . . . to
dance . . .

*(up on the Yiddish tune "Zetz" by Annie
Lubin [or some spirited klezmer tune or
Yiddish song from the '20s/'30s] as the
Librarian exits the stage, with the
Baedekers in his hand)*

THE END

Afterword

A spot of grocery shopping, a few diapers changed, dinner, a chat on the phone, a shower, a shave, and an arduous mission retrieving a small round dog toy from under the couch—that has been my day today, and all in all, little to write home about, certainly nothing demanding deep consideration, nothing out of the ordinary, nothing strange. That is, if it weren't for three incontrovertible Facts: 1) The universe contains well over 500,000,000,000 galaxies, with each galaxy containing over 1,000,000,000,000 stars, of which, our vast, blazing and life-bestowing sun . . . is one. 2) The Earth is 4,600,000,000 years old, in which time, from the Pre-Cambrian Era to the Present—a dizzying, terrifying number of inhabitants—amoebas and trilobites, dust mites and Neanderthals–have all struggled to live from one hour to the next. (Indeed, more living creatures are in my stomach—and yours—at this moment than the total number of human beings that have ever existed.) 3) I will die. I will be dead in sixty years, though it's entirely conceivable that I'll be dead before the week is out.

And suddenly all the props holding up my warm and secure little existence are kicked away and used for kindling. The imagination is taxed to exhaustion and left numb and agape when it even begins to fathom the implications of these Facts. They beggar the most breathless hyperbole. Three simple Facts, three confirmed and undeniable Facts—the immensity of the universe, the incomprehensibly vast history of the Earth, and our inescapable mortality—loom over all of us like three paisley mastodons. When I shine these three Facts upon any moment in my life, suddenly nothing, absolutely nothing, isn't strange, bewildering, and out of all whooping. These Facts turn every memorable or trivial or utterly forgettable moment of my existence—shopping, eating trout with spouse, lying prostrate retrieving dog toy— into the Apotheosis of the Comic and Tragic, the Inconsequential and Crucial, the Banal and Profound. These Facts loom so large, in fact, that they are rather easily ignored. Three paisley mastodons get up with us in the morning and sleep with us at night, but, for the most part, they're very quiet pachyderms, and consequently, amazingly, they blur into the unimportant background, even though one day, with trumpeting bellows, they will trample me into oblivion. Time and again I explain to myself that these Facts are interesting, profound even, but not pertinent to my daily life. NO. In truth, everything else is but shadow compared to these Facts. They are the trump cards to all the ordinary cards I hold in my hand and call "my life."

I write plays to help me keep these Three Facts

in the front of my head. In other words, I write to try to keep myself engaged with the Bewildering and Infinite. But why did I write *Underneath the Lintel* in particular?

All my plays are first inspired by music, and *Underneath the Lintel* was inspired particularly by certain klezmer/Yiddish music from the 1920s (and earlier). The "jaunty melancholy," the "dancing-despite-it-all" quality it contained, the defiance even—a certain "finding-joy-despite-all-the-evidence-to-the-contrary" quality in the music—compelled me to try to express it as a play.

In 1976, in Laetoli, in Tanzania, some members of Mary Leakey's archaeology team were throwing chunks of dried elephant dung at each other (as archaeologists are wont to do). When one of the paleontologists dived to the ground to avoid being pelted by dung, he noticed fossilized footprints of an animal, left in hardened volcanic ash from 3.8 million years ago. After two years of excavation, all number of animal prints were discovered, including, unexpectedly, unmistakably, the footprints of hominids—our ancient australopithecine ancestors. The fact that these prints were preserved— prints by an anonymous ancestor going about a no-doubt everyday activity—testifies to me of a great Conundrum of History: What is saved, and what is lost?

There used to be a sequence in *Underneath the Lintel*, which I considered and then excised before the New York production. After the Librarian points out the words on the moth's wing, and calls them a "ghostly vestige," he mentions how "vestige" comes from the Latin word "vestigium," meaning "footprint." The Librarian then alludes to the footprints left by our ancestors in Laetoli, and (unbeknownst to the Librarian) we see a slide of those Laetoli footprints, and then a subsequent fifteen-second slideshow depicting the subsequent four-million-year history of Humankind, full of our best and worst, and ending with a picture of a footprint left by the first man on the moon.

I loved the idea, and it looked really horrible when we actually tried to execute it, and then I hated the idea. So the sequence is out. But hopefully the idea can still be found in the play. "Still, we'll proceed," the Librarian says over and again, somehow we'll proceed, we haven't a choice, and perhaps such a sentiment has somehow driven the evolution of humanity itself, in tiny steps. Oh yes, we'll often go sideways or backwards, but continue we will, and perhaps "there is joy, too, in that."

What, after all, do we do with the fact that suffering has dogged humanity (and certainly not just humanity, but the three billion-odd species that have populated this planet) every step of the way? Calculated cruelty as well as utterly random events—ten million die in the senselessness of World War I and a woman is struck down by a frozen block of urine. The fact that we die is a great fat conundrum, and it will continue to be a conundrum for me until . . . well, until I die. What does my little life mean when set against the huge backdrop of human history? And what's human history set against the ridiculously unimaginable backdrop of the history of the universe? (At the Rose Planetarium in New York, there's a walk representing the history of the observable universe and at the end of the walk, there's a single hair, representing the 50,000 years of human existence). And what do we do with the fact that because we only live our lives once, a single event, or a single mistake, can send our lives into a wholly unanticipated and undesired direction?

So it was while I was listening to the klezmer music, and trying to think of a dramatic structure that would allow me to encompass a lot of history (in lieu of the Three Facts), that I remembered the story of the Wandering Jew. Now I was quite aware that the myth of the Wandering Jew was originally an anti-Semitic tale, but the myth had taken on more complex meanings in its seven-hundred-odd-year history, and I felt, besides, that an artist can always appropriate myths for his own ends. (I would later discover that a film made in Yiddish by Jews in the early '30s called *The Wandering Jew* was made to warn a generally ignorant world of the growing Nazi menace. In the film, the Wandering Jew is depicted as a noble figure, bearing witness to history. I've received letters calling *Underneath the Lintel* anti-Semitic. That said, I've also received letters calling the play too "pro-Zionist," and also "anti-Christian," for the portrayal of a cruel Christ, I suppose. So go figure.)

The first performance of *Underneath the Lintel* in New York was scheduled for September 18, 2001. The Soho Playhouse, being in Soho, was inaccessible for a week after the 11th, but we invited the neighborhood to see the show on the 19th. Yet although the events of 9/11 were singular and tragic, they were not, unfortunately, so out of the ordinary, when one considers the whole of history. On September 11, people were murdered out of anger and ignorance— victims who didn't want to die, and weren't expecting to die just then.

Afterword

Considered in this light, such events occur on larger and smaller scales *every day*, and have been occurring every day for thousands of years.

In a sense, despite the Wandering Jew's seemingly unique situation, his predicament is the predicament of all humanity—he made a mistake, a single mistake "underneath the lintel," when he put fear and self-interest ahead of compassion. Everyone does it all the time. And he was forced to live with that mistake the rest of his days. Did the punishment fit the crime? No. But that's often true of punishments and crimes. And even though he was condemned to live for a near-eternity, the fact that he is not allowed to be anything more than a myth (by not being allowed to communicate his existence to his fellow man) puts him in practically the same spot as the rest of humanity; namely, that his life means seemingly next to nothing in the great scope of history.

However, he is a human being, and he isn't going to give up so easily. Humanity inevitably finds the strength, despite our mistakes and tragedies, to rebuild, to persevere, to proceed, until death does us in. Graffiti throughout the ages (in a Lascaux cave or on a New York subway train) testifies to the fundamental human need to affirm our own existence to each other and to the Heavens. For our Librarian, the scraps left behind prove that the alleged Wandering Jew will never stop seeking "a way around" God's edict. And if the Wandering Jew has been condemned by God to witness thousands of years of human suffering, then, almost in defiance, he will seek out all that is good and worthy and beautiful, and if he is forced to "walk," he'll do God one better and Dance. Which of course, God no doubt wanted all along. This is the defiance, sadness, and hope I found expressed so fully in the klezmer music I had been listening to.

The Librarian made a mistake underneath the lintel—sending the one girl he ever loved away. His ensuing, long-sublimated spiritual crisis feeds his determination to find meaning in the clues he uncovers. But my point isn't that we should all believe in the Wandering Jew, or even in God, for that matter. Rather, anything at all—for the Librarian it was an impossibly overdue book—can be an invitation to the miraculous. And also this: That in the face of overwhelming existential bewilderment and terrible suffering, to respond with a little defiant dancing (in all its myriad forms) is a very human and very wondrous thing.

On one end of a spectrum is Coincidence, on the other end Profound Serendipity. The only difference between the two is how much meaning we choose to ascribe to a particular event. I'm still working out where on the spectrum I should put the following:

A few months back, I was paging through an encyclopedia of philosophy when I came across the word "sublime," which is defined as "the presence of transcendent vastness or greatness . . . While in one aspect, it is apprehended and grasped as a whole, it is felt as transcending our normal standards of measurement ... It involves a certain baffling of our faculty with feeling of limitation akin to awe and veneration; as well as a stimulation of our abilities and elevation of the self in sympathy with its object."

The word "sublime" comes from "sub" (*under*) + "limen" (which, like "limit," is a word derived originally from ... "*lintel*").

Though we rarely recognize the place, underneath the lintel is where we stand every day, every moment, of our lives.

—Glen Berger
New York, 2002